I0462796

THE GUIDE TO REHABBING HOUSES

Learn How to Rehab Residential Properties When Flipping

ANTONY PEACEFUL

Table of Contents

Introduction

Real estate investment is a term that you may have heard individuals speak about at some point. Even if you have not, you most likely have seen TV shows about flipping houses. For a lot of people, it is an easy strategy for making cash. Perhaps you have a close friend or relative who seems to make lots of profit from real estate, or the shows you have seen triggered your interest. Regardless of the situation, you now have an interest in the venture but have no idea where to start.

The truth is, there have been a lot of people in a similar situation as you. Worse still, a lot of them failed when they finally ventured into the business, while others took the right steps and attained success. So, what separates these sets of people? Why did some fail where others succeeded? How can you become one of those people who have succeeded?

Here's the good news: you have already taken an excellent first step, just by purchasing this book. This book will teach you everything you should know about rehabbing properties and real estate investment. You will also learn how to locate rehab deals and how to get the financing you require among a range of other vital information.

Now, let's begin this trip to becoming a successful property rehabber.

Chapter 1: Rehabbing Basics

Rehabbing or House flipping has gotten more popular over the years. In recent times, we have seen the rise of house flipping shows and experts in real estate investment on TV shows. This kind of real estate investment is advertised as being a leading method of getting a considerable amount of cash during a short period.

For a lot of individuals, rehabbing or house flipping is an excellent way of taking charge of their lifestyle and finances. There were moments when more than 250,000 rehabbers in the US were in search of properties to purchase and sell once more for profit. Also, official figures prove that during moments with the most activity, about 10 percent of all property sales have been flips.

However, if you watch reality shows a lot, you will know that it is not all reality. So what is rehabbing or house flipping? How does it work? We will be exploring all of these questions in detail in this chapter.

House Flipping: What is it?

House flipping is when an investor in real estate, purchases properties or homes and then disposes of them for a profit after making the essential repairs. For a home or property to be classified as a flip, it needs to be purchased to resell fast. The duration between when the property is bought and when it is sold usually falls within a few weeks and sometimes as long as a year.

There are various ways of flipping homes which we will be looking into below:

Fix and Flip or Rehabbing

This method of flipping homes is the most recognized one to date. It is the one you come across on television showing the purchase, fix, and flip technique of investing in residential properties.

Here, a real estate investor purchases a distressed home for a reasonable price. Then, he/she begins to carry out repairs on various aspects of the house, enhancing them and even replacing some components entirely. The instant they are through with repairs, they place the newly completed home on the market for sale with the hope of disposing of it for a higher price quickly.

If you are in search of a fast way to profit from real estate, this can be an excellent strategy to adopt. Also, this strategy can provide a valuable service to buyers, sellers, local neighborhoods, and the economy.

However, there are still other ways to fix and flip or rehab; investors in Fix and flip or rehabbers can differ depending on the level of fixing they intend to carry out on a property. Some investors don't go beyond some necessary cosmetic enhancement or looks. It is easy to enhance the value of a home and get more profit just by improving its appeal, which may consist of making a few renovations to the landscape. In contrast, some investors will stick to the basic painting of the exterior and interior of the property, installing new flooring, and replacing some fixtures.

Some other investors may choose to flip or rehab homes or properties with structural problems. These could range from replacing things like plumbing, foundations, roofs, and electrical wiring, among others. Properties that have these kinds of issues often come at a much lower price because of the increased risks and costs. Because of the low amount of competition involved in properties like these, some investors see this as a great option. However, many other investors stay away from them because of the additional capital requirements and liability.

All of these are great strategies for making a profit depending on your experience and the level of risk you are comfortable taking on. However, as a starter to the business of rehabbing homes, a safe bet for you would be to purchase a home that has the least issues. Doing this will allow you to fix and sell for a profit quickly.

Hold and Flip

Some investors are not interested in doing that much work, or who don't need the cash fast. If you fall into this category, this option will be ideal for you. Here, investors purchase a property and hold on to it till they can sell it for a profit later on. This could range from a day, months, or years. Investors who fall in this category are mostly depending on earning profit from a rise in price. This strategy comes with a lot of risks but can yield a lot of returns if it goes the right way.

Real Estate Wholesaling

Wholesaling is another method of house flipping. Here, you don't have to rehab or fix anything. It mostly involves purchasing properties at a low price and selling them for profit. Here, you sell most of these properties to rehabbers who do all the fixing before they sell it to the final users from the public who live in them or rent them out.

In this book, we will be paying attention to the first kind of house flipping called rehabbing or fix and flip. Now, let's have a look at how it works.

How Does a Real Estate Rehab Work?

Flipping homes typically has to do with purchasing a property or home to dispose of it for a profit. However, it is not as straightforward as that as there are a few factors involved.

- You need to make lots of choices from the start. For instance; where should you purchase? If you buy a property in a neighborhood that is just growing, you are hoping that the value of the area will go up. House flipping has a lot to do with the real estate market as well, for example; when there is a boom, it is an excellent market for rehabbers or flippers, and they can choose their prices in specific areas. However, when it is a slow period, a lot of these properties can remain on the market for a long time after they have been fixed.

- After deciding where you want to purchase

the property, you need to determine the kind of property you intend to buy. If you go with a property that is depreciated, you will need to make the necessary renovations which require money and time. If you decide to purchase from a bank or auction, you may get a good deal. However, you need to note that there may be hidden issues to deal with as well. We will be covering more on these later in this book.

- The next step is to go in pursuit of a way to finance your flip. This means you will search for lenders who can offer you the funding you require, depending on the property's value. If you can afford it, you can use your funds during this process.

- Once financing is in place, what you need to do next is make the necessary repairs to the home. To ensure this is a success, it is essential to pick the right contractors, stay within your budget and timeframe, and keep track of the repair cost, all in a bid to ensure you develop homes that individuals will want to purchase. Also, you have to learn to properly negotiate with contractors and pay them the appropriate amount, which will make sure that they do an excellent job for you.

- Finally, if you did all you were supposed to the right way, you will be left with a property people will love to buy. Here, you learn to advertise your property, and you sell it off at a profit.

Is House Flipping a Great Investment?

House flipping may seem like something simple, but it is not without its hassles. Speaking factually, if you flip a home the wrong way, it could lead to a massive amount of losses.

However, if you do it appropriately, a house flip can be a fantastic investment. In a brief period, you can make strategic repairs and dispose of the home for higher than you purchased it for. If you make the choice of flipping a house, your goal will certainly not be to lose your hard earned cash. You need to invest smartly so you can get the best Return on Investment.

Now that you understand how great an investment house flipping can be, you may be tempted to head right into it and start making a profit. However, this is not possible as you need to have a few things in place before you begin.

Requirements for House Flipping

To begin the business of house flipping, there are a few essentials you need. They include:

Good Credit Score

It will be challenging to start flipping houses if your credit is not great. At some point, you will require some form of loan unless you have enough money of your own to purchase a home and do all the needed repairs. The standards for lending have become stricter, especially if you are after a loan for a house flip which comes with a lot of risks.

If you don't know your score, the first thing you need to do is to find it. To get your credit record for free, click here. If your credit is not presently great, you need to begin developing your credit score by reducing your debts, paying bills at the right time, and ensuring the balance on your credit cards are low. There are various ways to do this, so ensure you do your research and do all you can to make your credit score better.

A better credit score will ensure the interest rates you get when you request a loan, will be much better. This can reduce a lot of cash from your expenses when you begin flipping homes, allowing you to invest more money in other vital areas.

Finally, you need to learn what makes your credit score go down. For example, when you take out a lot of credit cards simultaneously, it reduces your score. You have to ensure you stay away from activities that will bring your score down during the periods you apply for a loan.

Cash

Flipping a home requires capital. Lots of new investors run into financial issues when they initially purchase a property without a reasonable down payment, then use credit cards for the payment of renovations and home enhancements. If the property spends too much time on the market, or the cost of improvements is higher than projected, the investor may become stuck.

You want to do all you can to ensure this is not the case with you. If you're going to flip the right way, you will require a reasonable amount of money on hand. Lots of traditional lenders will need a 25% down payment, and they offer you the best rates you can find. When you have ample resources to make the down payment, you will eradicate the need to pay a PMI or private mortgage insurance which can take a dip into your returns.

In addition, the interest rates on loans for house flipping are higher than typical loans. As stated by

TIME, many investors request for an interest-only loan, which has a standard interest rate of 12- 14 percent. In contrast, the interest rate for conventional home loans is usually around 4 percent. The higher the amount of money you pay in cash, the lower the interest you will need to pay, which is why it is essential to have as much cash as possible on hand.

Why Should You Invest in House Flipping?

There is a range of benefits associated with flipping homes. You, as an investor, has the most to gain. For one, you get to earn a sizable amount of income if you know what you are doing. Even though the money you earn from flipping a property can differ based on a range of factors, in the end, what you make is better than you will get from working for someone else.

Also, the flexibility of the business means you can determine your work hours. You can decide to flip part-time or full-time, depending on what suits you best. You can decide to flip homes only during the weekends, or a few hours of the week after your typical work hours. Regardless of the option you choose to go with, you still retain full control of your scheduling.

You can take breaks when you want and close for the day when you desire, to spend more time with your family or attend important events. It gives you the chance to be your boss. You don't report to anyone but yourself, and it lets you take charge of your financial future.

House flipping also offers a range of benefits to all the parties involved. Similar to constructing a new home from scratch, rehabbing properties can create jobs for lots of people. It can also make revenue for the local government. What's more, a rehabbed home can enhance the value of a street or neighborhood.

Buyers and sellers can also enjoy some benefits as well. Many homeowners in dire need of cash, may be stuck in a financial crisis. When a real estate investor comes to take their property off their hands, it can help them get out of their financial crisis. Other individuals who want to purchase a residential home to live in may not buy those that are not structurally sound, require minor repairs, or have issues with the titles. Finally, buyers of homes also benefit because they can purchase properties they genuinely desire. Now that you understand how house flipping can be of benefit to you, the next chapter will be taking a look at the steps in a successful rehab.

Chapter 2: Steps in Rehabbing Houses

The business of rehabbing real estate can offer you a lot of profit and help you take charge of your finances. However, this venture can sometimes be a complex one. Nonetheless, if you have a deep understanding of the house flipping process and what a rehabber has to do from start to finish, you will be one step closer to achieving considerable returns from your investment. Also, you will have knowledge of real estate investment that will prove vital later down the road.

In this chapter, we will be taking a more in-depth look into the steps involved in a property rehab, which will ensure your investment journey is a less complex one. As with most things you need to do, the very first step is to make preparations.

Make Preparations

To be a successful rehabber, you need to learn about numerous areas of expertise. Some of these range from:

- The costs and process involved in a real estate rehab

- Transfer of Title

- How to evaluate properties

- Marketing real estate

- Partnership tax law among a host of others

Learning all the legal, physical, and financial aspects involved in a home rehab will be of positive impact to you down the road. Knowing all of these will help you enhance profits and curb any unneeded expenditure that may arise.

You will need to learn how to do proper diligence on a property before purchase, determine all of the costs that may come up and what you will spend on the actual property rehab itself. You need to plan by understanding all of these before you need them, so you know what to expect when the time comes. This is why it is vital to learn and make all your preparations before anything else. Even if you cover this, without proper knowledge of your market before you purchase a home, you can still end up taking a loss.

Understand Your Market

You need to know and understand your market. This means understanding the enhancements that are vital for a specific neighborhood and those that will make it more distinct and appealing even before you make a purchase. By researching the market, you will understand the core areas to invest your money in, which will draw in the most prospects specific to your chosen neighborhood. Modern bathrooms and kitchens are a trendy attraction in most real estate markets. In addition, buyers are attracted when these parts of the home are well organized and fitted with the most modern finishes. Understand what works for your market, so you know where to invest when the time comes.

Develop the Scope of Work

Your scope of work is where you list out every aspect of your project, down to the minor repairs. Doing this will ensure everyone involved will know what he/she is meant to do. To successfully achieve this, you need to:

- Make a detailed budget. Categorize your renovations as *Vital* or *Optional*

- Make a cost estimate for every project. Remember that you can let go of those that are optional if it goes past your set budget

- Outline everything you have to do for the property. This includes every renovation and repair down to the smallest pieces of furniture or fixtures. Here, you can also determine those materials you can use again as opposed to purchasing new ones.

- Add a projected cost of every project. Don't forget to plan for unforeseen expenses.

When you are through with your scope of work, make a final version which you will offer to your prospective contractors, so they know exactly what you want. After putting together your scope of work, you need to determine where your funding is going to come from.

Look for Investors or Finance

Locating funds is a major factor that stops many investors from becoming successful. For this reason, you need to determine where you will get the funds to finance your first house flip deal. So where can you locate individuals that will go on this journey with you? You can find many investors in networking events and REIA meetings, among others. Better still, you can try a hard money lender or a private lender. No matter the option you decide to go with, having a group of investors willing to finance your deal is vital to your success. Once you have sorted out your financing, the next thing you need to do is gather a team of professionals for your deal.

Get Your Team Together

To attain success, you need to keep a team of reliable professionals close by. A professional can aid in minimizing your expenses by connecting you with their networks. When you work alongside a team of professionals who know what they are doing, the house flip will be less complicated and will go more smoothly.

A general contractor is a vital addition to your team. He/she will play a considerable role during the renovation process. Next, you need an excellent realtor with the appropriate license. His access to Real Estate Owned inventory lists will be of great help to you in the long run. You will also need title agents or real estate attorneys to ensure the transfer of titles is as seamless as possible.

A rehab lending contact is also essential, particularly one who can deal with credit issues. Lastly, an accountant that can keep track of expenses and deal with taxes is also crucial.

Developing a team that can help with the process of rehab and marketing is of great significance for the short and long term success of your venture. Adding the right professionals in your network can ensure you remain on route to profit and success. After putting together a team, the next step is to find the right property to fix or rehab.

Find the Right Home to Rehab

The instant you have determined your scope of work and source of financing, the next step is to begin identifying the appropriate properties you can flip which will make you profit. Here, you need to put your timeline and budget into consideration and don't forget that no matter how well structured your plan is, it is still of utmost importance to locate the right property to yield the projected returns. Your major point of focus should be the neighborhood because you can always get a new property, but once you pick an area, you can't change it.

When choosing the appropriate property to flip, the following are a few vital factors to consider:

- Location of the Neighborhood: Pick a place that is not far from where you work and reside. This is because you may have to head to the site many times and you don't want to spend all of your profit on fuel or transportation.

- Properly Maintained Neighborhood: It is easy to enhance the look of your property. However, if the neighborhood is one that is not maintained correctly, there will be nothing you can do about it, and you may end up chasing off prospective buyers.

- Proximity to Amenities: Choose a neighborhood that is close to amenities like libraries, parks, shopping, and restaurants. This will help draw buyers in and allow you to attach premium prices to your property.

- Research the Market: Find out how long properties stay on the market in the neighborhood. This will determine the duration of time you may have to wait to dispose of your property. If your aim is a quick turnaround, you will want to stay away from markets where properties sit for a long time before being purchased.

- Properties Without Structural Issues: Stay away from properties that have problems close to the foundation, no matter how good the deal may seem. This could include issues like sinking floors. You may end up spending way more than you anticipated correcting these issues, which may end up taking a bite into your projected profit.

- Size of the Property: Go for properties that are of decent proportions. You can break down walls to create more room inside the home, but it will be impossible to add additional space or a garden if there is no space to do so. Next, you need to run your numbers to determine if the investment is worth it.

Run Your Numbers

When investing in homes, you need to note that you are purchasing the property to make a profit and nothing else. The numbers should tell you how to proceed. Don't get attached to a home you want to rehab because you feel it is appealing or in a fantastic neighborhood.

You know the purchase price of your property, and you also understand the amount you are ready to invest in enhancement. However, it is also vital to determine closing and holding costs. You also need to determine the interest you owe on loans, insurance, property taxes, and title costs. This is particularly necessary during a flip where selling a property fast can be vital to your profit margin. Run the numbers and also allocate resources for unforeseen expenses.

After pointing out a property, you want to purchase, do your calculations and be sure you are making money off the venture. Always have a plan B in place, or a fast exit strategy in the event things do not go as planned.

Rehab

After purchasing the property, what you need to do is rehab or fix it. Be sure that the contractor you finally decide to work with is reliable and has the proper licenses. It is best to work with contractors you have had a prior relationship with or someone with excellent references. Always make yourself physically available during the project because no one else can keep track of how your money is being spent except you. If you are unavailable, feel free to delegate this to someone you can trust. However, you still need to make yourself available frequently during the rehab.

Also, exercise caution when choosing décor for the home. Don't go with what you like; instead, go with what is presently trending and is known to be alluring to lots of buyers. Your buyers have to find the home appealing, not you. If you rehab a property the right way, and no one knows of its existence, it may end up sitting on the market for a very long time without any buyer. That is why the next step of learning to market the property is equally important.

Market the Property

Fix a price, which is a little lower than market price to get fast foot traffic and interest. Don't let your greed take over when it comes to pricing because for every day the property sits on the market without a buyer; you are losing income. Take every step you can to market the property effectively. You can use flyers, list it online, provide a referral fee if someone brings you a buyer and so on. Most times, even if people don't want to purchase a home, they know others who would want to.

Create awareness right from when you are almost through with the rehab process. This will keep prospective buyers in anticipation even before the rehab process is complete. Place a sign in front of the home and do an open house. Be strategic with your promotion as many people purchase homes based on emotions. So advertise your home in a way that will trigger these emotions.

Stage the property as best as you can. Place furniture and tables and make anyone who walks in envision how the property would look as their home. If you are not very skilled at this, you can get the services of real estate agents around to help you out with this.

Flip the House

If you do everything the right way, you will be selling off your property for a profit in no time.

Having understood the steps in a rehab, let's move on to the best ways to find house flipping deals.

Chapter 3: How to Find Rehab Properties to Flip

Understanding the rehab process is just one step of the hurdle to becoming a successful rehabber. Another vital step is to know where you can search for properties at low prices which you can flip for a profit. In this chapter, we will be taking a look at some of the leading locations where you can find the best property rehab deals. For every new investor, the first and most comfortable place to start your search is the MLS.

Check out the (MLS) Multiple Listing Service

This is a database which consists of all the properties available for sale placed by listing agents representing sellers , and where the agents representing buyers, also known as buyer's agents, typically look for properties on behalf of their buyers. Contrary to popular belief, there is no single MLS. For every major city, there will be a MLS, while there are cities that have more than one MLS. Almost any kind of home for sale via a real estate agent will be listed on the MLS. This could include short sales, REOs, and retail sales. The market changes fast, and if you don't have more than one method of getting properties to flip, you will soon be without any earnings and no opportunity to locate additional homes to flip.

There are numerous benefits you stand to gain by using the MLS to find deals. First, the MLS requires minimal marketing effort on your end. A considerable percentage of the homes for sale can be found on the MLS, which means deals find you as opposed to the need of you marketing for them. This can aid you in saving a lot of cash on your marketing costs and also save you time in your other aspects of marketing.

Besides, if you depend on a real estate agent with access to the MLS to bring you deals, it won't cost you a thing which is another reason this is a great location to begin your search for deals, especially as a starter.

Become a part of Real Estate Groups

When you become a member of a Real Estate Group, you place yourself amidst the top players in real estate close to you. Also, when communicating with members of the group or picking up a real estate rehab project, there is a high possibility you will find someone working on a project which requires partners.

Furthermore, you may find out about a home an investor wants to let go of because they do not have the needed time on their hands to complete the flip. The same may also apply if they wish to channel their resources to other areas instead of the flip. You can also make valuable business connections and friends from many of these groups. To locate a Real Estate Group close to you, run a search on the internet using the keywords "real estate investment clubs," and a list of the groups in your area will pop up for you to make your choice.

Look into Tax Auctions

Sheriff's sales and Tax actions are ideal for finding rehab properties. They consist of homes being sold as a result of unsettled property taxes. It is possible to flip these kinds of properties, but there are a lot of risks associated with these kinds of properties. You need to be sure of what you are delving into with these kinds of properties and do comps (comparison with homes or properties in the same area as yours, with similar sizes and features) of your own, so you are assured of the ideal price to leave at the closing table.

However, you need to note that once you take ownership of the property, you will be required to settle all the prior taxes owed on the property. If you are unlucky, this may be a lot and could dip into your profit. To learn more about sheriff's sales and tax auctions, check out your city or county's website. Sales are carried out at a public auction, and buyers will need to place bids on properties to win them.

Collaborate with a Wholesaler

Wholesalers operate by locating properties to rehab, placing them on contract and finding an instant buyer who will replace the wholesaler and carry out the initial contract put in place. The investor or buyer then pays a fee to the wholesaler for playing the role of an intermediary. Even though this method of finding properties to flip is not the cheapest, it can be swift and save you lots of cash going forward. Many wholesalers locate properties to flip as a day job and have lots of connections in specific areas. They also have good relationships with particular sellers and agents. You can find many of these wholesalers in groups for real estate investment.

After getting a property, wholesalers often include some description of the product. To find wholesalers, you can run a search on your search engine with the keyword "real estate wholesalers," and you will be greeted with lots of options to choose from. However, wholesalers only like to work with individuals with cash or asset-based loans which have already been approved.

Go Through the Local Paper

For many, this option may seem obsolete. However, there are lots of people who still advertise properties to sell in the local paper. You will probably come across lots of ads for open houses, but the sale price and the location is also usually listed. However, with the enhancements in technology, the local paper might be a very stressful and time-consuming place to search for deals. Nonetheless, this does not mean they are not a great way to find properties to flip.

Purchase Lead Lists

Lead lists are a well-known technique used by property investors to generate leads. They consist of information on various things ranging from foreclosure prospects, expired listings, divorces, deaths, and other situations that portray that a homeowner may want to sell.

However, the information you find from this lead is not usually current, which means there is a high possibility of reaching people that have already been contacted by other local investors. This could trigger frustration instead of interest in homeowners, mainly if they are not happy about their present state. This option should be one of the last ones on your list.

Run Adverts

If you have the time, expertise, and funds, running ads to homeowner directly can aid them in locating you as much as it assists you in finding them. There are a few vital marketing tools investors can use for their advertisement campaigns like radio ads, billboards, TV commercials, and direct mail. Taking advantage of social media platforms can also bring about some considerable benefits to your ad campaigns.

On the downside, regardless of the kind of advertising you decide to go with, it can cost you a substantial amount of cash. If you don't have the time or capacity to develop an ad campaign on your own, you can get the services of an expert to do it on your behalf. Also, it requires time to establish a presence that connotes trust in the marketplace, even if you have been able to develop a great campaign. When you are just starting the business of rehabbing homes, this may be time that you don't have to spare. Nonetheless, this is still an excellent method of finding properties to rehab.

Reach out to the Offices of County and City Assessors

A majority of the county and city tax assessor's offices have a list of homes which owe back taxes. If you can bring any of the taxes up to date and pay off the fees and interest that have accrued, you will have the capacity to charge a considerable rate of interest. If the homeowner is unable to redeem these taxes within a stipulated period, you will also get ownership of the property. No matter how it goes, you will have the chance to earn some cash on interest and possibly more on profit if you can gain ownership of the property.

However, you need to do investigations of your own to locate the properties that have been failing to meet their taxes, and it is not an easy feat to achieve on the websites of some cities or counties. Also, you won't get the chance to do a home inspection before you gain full ownership of the property if this is ever the case. In the end, you could be stuck with a money drainer that could take a dip into your possible returns.

Go Through Government Agency Sites

Government agencies that insure mortgages or offer loans to homeowners also have the capacity to foreclose on properties similar to how traditional lenders would if the loan does not get paid. By going through the sites for every government agency, you may be able to locate foreclosed properties which they want to let go of at reduced prices.

However, the drawback is that every agency works on its own and has its own set of rules guiding the purchase of their properties. In essence, in addition to searching or properties available for purchase on numerous websites, you also need to understand the rules and regulations of various government agencies. This may end up consuming a lot of time you could have channeled to other areas.

Look into Estate and Probate Sales

This is another fantastic method of locating properties in reasonable shape at reduced prices. Probate sales is a situation where the probate court sells properties because the owners did not put a will in place before their demise or had no heirs. This is like an advanced method of getting homes to flip, but it can be highly beneficial once you know the risks.

Getting properties from a probate sale comes with its drawbacks. First, you have to place a non-refundable 10 percent deposit. This means if you are unable to close the sale, you forgo these deposits. In addition, sellers are not obligated to disclose any defects to the properties, which means you may purchase a home which requires a lot of repairs making it more of a money drainer than a good deal. Lastly, until you have closed and gotten under contract, the property will keep on being marketed, which means you need to be prepared to deal with counter-offers by matching or topping them.

Reach Out to Absentee Homeowners

If you come across a property that is not well-taken care of, and you feel it may have been placed on rent, you can head to your town clerk to locate the owner's name. In addition, check out the obituary category of newspapers to get leads on properties that may be listed on the market due to the demise of a cherished family member. Then offer to buy the property by sending a letter.

You can check out https://www.whitepages.com/ to find where absentee homeowners stay. You can also locate individuals who have inherited homes via the website above.

Collaborate with Lawyers to find House flipping Deals

- Collaborate with probate lawyers: Probate lawyers always work alongside families dealing with the probate process to liquidate properties like stocks, vehicles, houses, among others to share among the living heirs. Nurturing relationships with probate lawyers can offer you access to a range of opportunities without competition in purchasing the property. Most times, families want to dispose of assets in the estate as fast as they can to get their inheritance. The great part of this is; you have a seller who is very motivated, and you can capitalize on the urge they have to sell quick, by purchasing the property at a hugely discounted cost if you are able to close quickly. It can also work to your benefit if the lawyer is on your side to give them a little push.

- Collaborate with divorce Lawyers: It is common knowledge that individuals dealing with a divorce tend to be a little vindictive and illogical. Most times, some individuals do not bother about what they get so long as the other individual involved does not get as much. Most times, there is usually a home which you can flip for profit after a divorce.

- Collaborate with Bankruptcy Lawyers: These lawyers will have individuals they are working with, filing for bankruptcy who may be eager to dispose of their homes before filing or after they file. Even though this is sad news for individuals filing for bankruptcy, these kinds of lawyers can offer you leads that are likely to be profitable. In addition, you can check out the local newspaper for bankruptcy sales because there is an obligation to post a notice before any sale as a result of bankruptcy.

- Collaborate with real estate lawyers: Real estate attorneys work in fixing issues individuals are facing in their joint ventures and partnerships among others. This is in addition to their roles in treating real estate closings. What this means is, they will know about real estate deals that were unable to close for numerous reasons, and you can make yourself available to provide the seller with a juicy offer.

Now, you know where to find the best deals or at least good leads. However, if you don't have your financing in place, you won't be able to afford the property when you find a property you like. For this reason, you need to learn ways to get financing, and we will be covering this in the chapter to follow.

Chapter 4: Getting Your Financing in Place

According to research, it was observed that in 2017, over 200,000 homes were renovated by home flippers, who earned a typical profit of $68,143 on each property (Prakash, 2019). This is a vast amount of cash and a lot of houses. Even with the high level of popularity of house flipping, one of the major constraints lots of people tend to deal with is cash. If you don't have adequate funds, you will be unable to buy a home, carry out renovations, get a team, or locate a buyer for the home or property when you want to sell.

On the bright side, there are numerous options to find funding for your rehab deal, letting you buy your property quickly and start your project. Even as a starter or an experienced rehabber, you can take advantage of the various flipping options to move further in the business of real estate investment.

In this chapter, we will be covering all you need to know about getting funding and the various options available to you. But before moving any further, let's take a look at what rehab loans are.

About Rehab Loans

After locating a property, you will need to determine how you will fund your flip. And if you are not extremely wealthy, it will be essential to borrow some cash to finance some core aspects of your house flip, some of which include:

- Paying the purchase cost of the property: You have to make a 20 percent down payment or more of the property depending on your lender

- The property's holding cost, which includes HOA fees, insurance payments, and other costs that come with being the owner of the home while doing renovations.

- Labor and other materials you will use for renovation

- Closing costs to locate a buyer and dispose of the property after renovation

- Realtor costs

Before you look for funding for your house flip, you need to bear in mind that traditional bank loans should be your last option. As a real estate rehabber, your income may not be consistent, and many banks would not be keen on offering you a loan to flip properties. Also, even if a bank decides to work with you, they may not offer you a loan product that will be ideal for your requirements. What is more, bank loans are usually not short-term loans, and as a real estate rehabber who purchases, fixes, and disposes of properties within a short while, this may not be a good option.

Because bank loans are not easy to get, may rehabbers always search for other sources. As a newbie, you can request a loan from your family and friends. Other flippers capitalize on other options like dipping into home equity. The instant you have an excellent record of successfully flipping homes, you will have better access to more sources of funding. Below, we will be taking a more in-depth look at the options available to you.

Loans from Family and Friends

Your personal network is an excellent location to begin your search for real estate rehab funding. Your friend, brother, your sister's friend, or cousin could end up as a great source of financing. Many individuals invest in real estate deals to get returns higher than what is offered on the market, and for this reason, they may have an interest in your project. In addition, because you know your friends and family members personally, they could offer you the least interest rates.

Just like you would when getting loans from other sources, you need to adhere to a few rules when taking loans from your those who fall in this category. The first step is to ensure that you outline all of the terms and conditions of the loan in writing. Here, you will write down the date you are to pay, and the amount of interest. A written document, aside from showing the seriousness of your intention to pay, also safeguards all parties involved. The next step is to ensure that you are in line with all the securities laws and IRS laws that regulate family investments.

The terms of your property rehab loan will be dependent on the loan size, the property specs, your flipping experience, your geographic market, and the amount of risk the lender is willing to take. Typically, the borrower does not make any payment during renovating the home, but after the house has been sold, he/she pays back all borrowed funds with the agreed interest. The borrower also places the home as collateral in the event he/she fails to pay back the loan.

Source for A Financing Partner

Some flippers have an excellent market knowledge

and the ability to spot great opportunities to flip homes; however, they do not have the resources to complete the project. In situations like this, collaborating with a partner can be helpful.

Partners can help with the following:

- Locating the house to flip

- Planning and overseeing the renovation

- Providing finance

The profit is split between both partners, depending on what they are bringing in. Usually, a partner manages the renovation and locates the opportunity to flip while the other offers the needed finance. You can stick with one partner for numerous projects or change partners for each project.

The amount the partner who provides funding can get after the sale is dependent on the kind of negotiations they carry out with the other partner, and if they are bringing other things on board. If the funding partner is only bringing the funding and no other thing, they usually get around 33 to 50 percent of the returns. However, the same also applies if there is a loss as opposed to a profit. When this occurs, the loss is also shared by all the partners.

Similar to loans from family and friends, it is ideal to put everything down in writing, usually known as a partnership agreement. You can get an attorney to help you put together this partnership agreement, but if it is not complicated, numerous DIY legal websites can aid you in putting one together yourself.

Line of Credit or Home Equity Loan

This is another conventional means of getting funding for rehab deals. If you are a homeowner, you can dip into the equity of your home. But this implies that you can only use this option if you have a home. A (HEL) home equity loan can offer you access to the financing you need to flip a home, and you can dip in for funds as you require. In addition, when you pay interest, you only do so on the cash you use. In contrast to a loan, a line of credit lets you borrow as much as you require until it gets to the limit.

The difference between the balance on your mortgage and your home's market value is the equity. To be eligible for a line of credit or equity loan, you need to have no less than 20 percent equity on your property. Depending on the amount of loan you need, it's better to have higher equity. Your credit also needs to be great, and you need to have a monthly income reasonable enough to ensure you can keep up with mortgage payments and clear off the home equity loan.

Lots of banks will give you loans as high as 85% of your primary residence property, after deducting the balance of your loan. If the money you get is inadequate to finish up your rehab project, you can merge this option of funding with other methods of finance. While interest rates are currently increasing, home equity loans still provide you with some of the lowest rates of interests available.

401(k) Financing

This is another excellent way to finance your real estate rehab. Here, you take out funds from your 401(k) account or take a loan from it. However, if you are close to the age of retirement, this option may not be ideal for you. On the other hand, if you a young rehabber, it may be a good idea to take from this account.

The majority of the 401(k) accounts provided by employers will give you the chance to request loans as high as 50% of the balance in your account. 401(k) plans for self-employed individuals also support loans of as much as $50,000. When repaying the loans, there is an interest attached. However, it is your money, and you are repaying all of the funds, including the interest to yourself.

In addition, some individuals request loans from their life insurance policy as a means of financing their house flip. This is almost like requesting a loan from your 401(k) account.

Personal Loans

This is a financing product with a lot of flexibility. Similar to a personal business loan, you can utilize the cash you get from these kinds of loans for anything you want, which includes a real estate rehab project.

To be eligible for this loan, you require a credit score of more than 650. Personal loans can come with rates as little as 5%, and you are allowed to spread out the payments over three to seven years. However, these loans are not much and have a $50,000 limit. So if you have a considerable rehab project, you may need to merge it with other financing options.

Seller Financing

This is also recognized as owner financing. It is a situation where the individual who wants to sell the home, plays the role of the lender. As opposed to taking a bank mortgage, or requesting loans from a lender, you request the seller to provide funding for the rehab deal. Many home sellers would want to have access to the cash they get from their home sale immediately. But, it may be a great idea to find out if the present owner has an interest in seller financing, particularly if they are keen on quickly disposing of the home. This form of financing offers benefits to the flipper and the homeowner.

Usually, the flippers pay off the interest alone until they can sell off the property. At this moment, they pay a considerable sum to the seller to offset all debts. The seller can put a specific date in place where the borrower would be required to pay off the loan. When the date is due, the borrower needs to dispose of the property or get another loan to offset what he/she owes the seller.

Same with other options we have covered so far, you need to put down the terms of this financing in writing. Because the seller is not someone you share a personal relationship with, it is advisable to call on a lawyer to help you create the loan papers.

Hard Money Loans

These are loans you get from private individuals or investors. The requirements to be eligible for these kinds of loans are not as high as a typical bank loan, and you can get the finance for this form of funding in two weeks or less.

Because hard money lenders offer loans to borrowers who are not qualified in terms of credit scores, the interest rate they charge is usually way more than other standard options. It is usually around 10 – 20%. Also, these lenders include fees too, resulting in an overall cost that is much higher than the original loan amount. This is the reason why it is best to try out other cheaper alternatives before you decide to go with hard money loans.

There are numerous online platforms and private loans lenders that deal in providing hard money loans to rehab homes. Some popular options include RealtyMogul and LendingHome. Hard money loans aim to help you stay afloat until you finish fixing the property and dispose of it. For this reason, there is a one-year cap attached to a typical hard money loan even though there are lengthier options available. Also, the down payment attached to hard money loans are not as high and are normally around 10%. This is because the lender is more interested in the property's potential as opposed to the borrower's background.

Once Hard money lenders approve your loan, they give you the loan in segments. First, they offer you cash to buy the home and do the first batch of renovations. When the contractor is through with the first set of renovations, they provide you funds for the next set and so on.

Business Line of Credit

When you have attained a successful house flipping record, you will get access to bank financing. Standard bank loans may not align properly with property rehab funding; however, business lines of credit can provide you the needed funding for a house flip. Using a line of credit, you will be privy to a precise amount of cash but will only need to pay for what you utilize. This makes it a great option when you don't know the amount you may need to carry out renovations on a property or the length of the renovation.

Business lines of credit are similar to home equity lines of credit, but the major distinction is the amount of cash you get. With business lines of credit, you can get as high as seven figures depending on your flipping experience and the income of your business.

You can head to your local bank to apply for a business line of credit. However, even though the interest rates are not high, you will require an excellent credit score of more than 700 to be eligible for this loan. You will also require a consistent history of income and a reasonable amount of cash in the bank.

Crowdfunding

This depends on a group of organizations or individuals to finance loans collectively. Every lender, who is called an investor, offers a little percentage of the loan required by the borrower and gets interest on that money. The usual crowdfunding websites like Prosper are not designed to provide loans for purchasing and flipping properties. The peak amount of loan you can get from a website like Prosper is $35,000 and is ideal for projects like debt consolidation and home renovation. However, specialty crowdfunding websites for rehabbers can be of help here.

Some of them will provide funding for your loan, which means that the organization will close your loan with its funds pending the period investors provide funding, while others don't close loans till investors have funded it entirely. This may mean no closing or slower closing. Similar to hard money lenders, crowdfunding websites do not care about the background of the borrower but are more interested in the quality of the property or collateral.

Conventional Mortgages

Lots of traditional mortgages are offered by banks with a requirement of no less than 20 percent down payments. In contrast, conventional mortgages have a low-interest rate, usually in the field of 5%.

These mortgages may be quite challenging to be eligible for. Banks often need:

- A credit score of more than 700

- No less than two years track record of real estate rehab deals with profit

- No recent foreclosures or bankruptcies

In addition, banks may take a while to approve loans because of their comprehensive process. As a rehabber who deals in fixing and flipping, this may be a drawback because of the fast pace of the real estate market. The instant an investor finds a property he/she deems profitable, many of them try to purchase it fast before another investor does.

If you have your financing in place, it does not mean you rush to purchase the first property you come across. Doing this can still result in you making losses even with adequate financing. Before you purchase a rehab property, you need to understand how to evaluate the cost of repairs on a rehab property and if it will bring you profit in the long run. The chapter to follow will further elaborate this.

Chapter 5: How to Evaluate the Cost of Repairs on a Rehab Property

When it comes to investing in real estate, including rehabbing properties, a very crucial aspect, is the capacity to evaluate the amount you will need to spend on a home to get it into a desirable state. This is not a skill that you can learn with ease. There are tons of tools that can aid you in evaluating the repair cost to a reasonable extent, but most of them usually result in you paying more than you need to. In this chapter, we will be looking into the steps to accurately evaluate a rehab property's cost of repair alongside other vital information. But first, why is it essential to accurately estimate the cost of repairs? Let us learn why below.

Why it is Crucial to Accurately Estimate Repair Costs

A typical mistake lots of new investors make is not accurately estimating the repair costs of a structure like re-plumbing, re-roofing, and cooling and heating system replacements alongside other enhancements like fixtures, new flooring, and paint.

Some investors overestimate the expenses that have to do with fixing a property which is equally as damaging as underestimating the expenses. Regardless of which you go with, you are going down a path of failure in your investment.

The reason is simple; if you underestimate the expenses of a home rehab, you will spend a lot of time doing rehab on the property, but you will learn that when you sell it off later, your profit won't be as much as you anticipated. Dealing with a loss like this can ensure you don't want to go into another rehab project, which could have been an ideal means for you to develop your wealth and take charge of your finances.

In the same light, overestimating how much a project costs, can lead to you making a bid which the seller may find too low to accept. It could also result in you losing the deal to a competing investor who made an accurate cost estimate and was able to outbid you. Not accurately evaluating repair costs may also make you let go of a property which could have brought you high profit. It is not easy to find good deals, so any opportunity you don't take advantage of can be very costly.

Can You Rely on Software for Evaluating Repair Costs of a Home?

For many new investors, the first location they head to for assistance in the evaluation of home repair costs is a tool on their computer. However, this may not be the right route to take. There is a range of amazing tools which contractors use in estimating how much a project costs; Nonetheless, they need you to:

- Understand the materials you will require to get the job done

- Know the cost of your materials from your chosen supplier

If you are a property rehabber making efforts to determine the overall cost you will need to renovate a home you are only in view of buying, these tools may end up seeming like guesswork. There are a few tools commonly used by new investors, but they do not do the work well enough.

One of these is XactRemodel, which is an online tool utilized by builders and insurance companies. The program provides an elaborate database of retail costs and construction costs for almost everything. But, unless you are ready to pay retail prices for materials as well as labor, this tool for estimating home repairs may not be useful for you.

Another popular option is The GeneralCost Estimator, a tool that offers standard prices categorized based on cities to develop a precise home estimate in your neighborhood. This software needs you to place every item in the spreadsheet to determine the cost of renovations. But if you have not entirely assessed the property and have an idea of what you need, the program is of no help.

Since software should not be the route you should take, a better option would be for you to get an expert to do an estimate of the job for you.

Getting The Help of a Professional

You need to be ready for a professional to charge you a fee for providing an estimate. The following are some of the charges you may be asked to pay:

- A trip charge which covers the expenses and time used in driving to the property

- Possibly an extra charge for fuel if the property is exceptionally far

- A diagnostic fee for assessment on any issue they can't see immediately

- A design fee for assessments on renovations

which go past typical repairs

- A service fee if you are offered an estimate and end up not hiring that contractor to carry out the job

Averagely, the professional estimate can fall around $50-$200 unless you get charged with an extra design fee. Renovation estimates can be more than five times repair costs estimate because designing something new is not so simple.

Things an Actual Estimate Should Include

When a proper estimate is offered to you by a professional, it needs to go beyond a projected number, you should look forward to paying. A quality estimate from a contractor should inform you about:

- The project scope, outlined so that it shows which subcontractor or contractor will be responsible for which areas of the project,

- The time it will require to finish the job

- The payment terms

- The cost of materials

- The cost of labor

- Permitting costs and other expenses that may come up

Also, every estimate should be followed with evidence of the license, which proves that the contractor is allowed to do contracting jobs, along with evidence of their bonding and insurance. It is also preferable that you are provided some proof or certification of their proficiency in their precise area.

The Right Process of Getting Estimates From Experts

There are appropriate steps to follow when you want to get estimates from professionals to get an outcome you can work with. Below, we will be taking a look at each of these steps.

Determine Your Financing

Before you begin to think of attaining an estimate for the repair cost of your property, you need to ensure you already have an amount you can spend in mind. Get approval for any loans beforehand, and if you can, make the deal dependent on you gaining access to these loans. Doing this will make sure you don't spend cash getting estimates from professionals you will end up not using. In addition, it will offer you a peak amount you can set your bid to the instant you have estimates ready. Once you have been able to put this in place, the next thing is for you to assess the property's structure.

Carry out a Structural Assessment of the Property if Required

If there is major damage to the structure of the building, you need to get the services of a structural engineer to analyze the house and offer you an assessment of the amount you will require to make the property livable. Nevertheless, structural engineers can be a bit on the high side, so be prepared to invest $500 or more to get this form of service. In most instances, its best you stay away from bidding on properties that have apparent damage, unless you have the experience and you are getting it for a hugely discounted price.

Run an Assessment of the Typical Risks

Many home inspectors will possess the tools to look for all the typical dangers of an ancient property. However, if your inspectors don't possess this skill, get the services of an expert to assess for:

- Dangerous Mold

- Lead-based paint

- Hidden pests

- Dangers of flood

- Issues with the well or septic system and

- Other typical dangers which are hidden but unique to your neighborhood

Do an Assessment of the Innards

This should consist of the results you can hope to get from a home inspector. It is a look at all the issues with the property's basic pieces. This could include:

- Insulation

- Foundation

- Roof

- Interior and exterior walls

- Doors and Windows

- Bathroom

- Flooring

- Electrical, HVAC and plumbing

- Exterior flatwork and concrete

- Trim and framing

- Closets and others

These are vital aspects of a property that must have been appropriately repaired before it can be deemed habitable. For this reason, it is essential for you to assess each one of these areas.

Assess the Specifics

The remaining specifics include areas you will always need to improve on a little before trying to sell or rent a property. However, you may want to deal with this on your own or with the assistance of hired individuals who are not as professional as complete contractors. Nonetheless, you need to include them in any of your estimates. They include:

- Interior and exterior paint

- Yard cleanup and landscaping

- Repair of garage

- Installation of appliances

- Chimney or fireplace

- Patio, porch or decks

The Completion

Finally, be sure that any bids you are offered consists of all the vital details needed for completing the repair of a property. Be sure to get costs for:

- Demolition

- Permits

- Disposal of garbage

- Staging, if required

By now, you may have begun to understand why getting a proper estimate is a bit pricey, and why it may take some time to complete. It is not convenient, and it is less complicated than depending on software-based tools. However, it is the best way for you to get a proper estimate of the repair costs of your home.

If there is a contractor who you know is reliable, and you have a good relationship with, request an estimate from him and go with it. If this is not the case, get an evaluation from more than one contractor, and make a comparison of the results they provide. However, this means you will spend three times the time and cash, but it is a great way to develop a standing relationship. It will also offer you an idea of the right estimates to go with, which can make the additional expenses worth it.

Be Ready for Costs to Change

A major lesson you will learn when it comes to flipping homes is that there will be times when an estimate you make will be lower as a result of unexpected repairs or issues that you did not see coming, while some more substantial costs you projected may end up being cheaper than your initial estimates.

The longer you retain ownership to a property before you sell it off means an increase in your costs like insurance, taxes, maintenance, and utilities. This means the quicker you get it done, the larger the profit you will earn. For this reason, it may be a great choice to purchase all the materials you can buy, but ensure you can return every item you purchase.

With the tips we have covered above, you can properly estimate the repair cost of a property, to ensure you are taking up a deal that will yield you returns. In addition to learning how to evaluate the costs of repairs on a property, it is also vital for you to understand some basic formulas that can help you stay in line and ensure you make a profit from your rehab deal.

Formulas to Learn for Flipping Homes

When it has to do with flipping a home, determining your numbers, as we covered earlier, is quite vital. If you aim to get the most profit from a property flip, it is essential to arm yourself with the formula which is used for flipping homes.

In this section, we will be looking into a few vital formulas you require if you want to become a success in this venture.

(ARV) After Repair Value Formula

The ARV is an estimate of a property's future value after all the needed repairs have been done. In essence, it is the value of a home after you have made your updates and upgrades.

Numerous factors can have an impact on your ARV calculation. However, there are two major areas which include the repair value and the cost of purchasing the home or property.

To calculate the ARV, the formula to use is: (Renovation Cost) + (Property Purchase Price)

70% Rule Formula

If you are not new to the business of flipping

properties, there is a huge chance that you may have heard of the formula which is called the 70% rule.

Here, you multiply the after repair value of a property by 70%, then minus the cost of repair. The balance you get is what you will require to buy a home if you want to make a reasonable amount of profit.

The formula for this rule is: (ARV x 70%) – Repair Cost.

When Can You Deviate from the 70% Rule?

If you are new to house flipping, it is not a great idea to deviate from this rule. But if the market you are in is extremely competitive, and it is required for you to provide an offer that is more than 70% to outbid the competition and get the deal, then don't hesitate to do this. There are a few cities which have serious competition, where you won't have the capacity to win a bid placed at 70%. In these kinds of neighborhoods, it may be a great choice to alter your numbers a little.

Maximum Purchase Price

This is a formula you will require to do an elaborate evaluation of the overall project costs after you have found out how valuable a home is with the 70 percent rule.

The formula for calculating this is ARV - Costs of Repair - Funding Costs - Selling Costs.

Expected Return on Investment

This is the amount you project you will make after selling a home. The more your return on the investment, the more profit you will make. This is the goal of every investment: High profit. If you have a low ROI, then the same applies to your profit as well. Your ROI is also impacted by your timelines, ARV, and budget.

To get the expected ROI, use this formula: Net Profit/Total Investment x 100.

The Offer Price Formula

This is the price you are ready to part with for a property. You have to exercise caution in this area, or you may end up paying a lot for a home. Your aim should be to provide an offer price that is of benefit to you and satisfactory to the seller as well.

Use this formula to get the offer price: ARV - (Renovation Cost + Holding and Closing Costs + Cost of Financing + Profit Target) = Offer price. Now that you understand how to evaluate costs and some of the vital formulas to note let's break down some of the core aspects of a property you need to inspect before purchase.

Essential Aspects to Inspect Before You Purchase a Property

Before you buy a property to flip, there are some key areas you need to inspect to ensure the property is structurally sound. Not inspecting these areas may result in you investing more cash than necessary into rehabbing a property which means fewer returns for you. Below, we will be delving into some of the vital areas you need to inspect before buying a rehab property.

Roof

From a glance, does the roof look good? Go closer to find out. Does the roof have worn shingles? Does the decking seem rotten and bowed? These are some of the things to take note of.

Windows

The windows are also critical. Look around for any damaged windows, and note the number you may have to purchase.

Foundation

Walk around the whole building, and take note of the structure close to the ground. Search for cracks, but not minor cracks as all buildings come with some little cracks. However, major cracks around the foundation should bother you.

Exterior Paint

Simply put, check out the exterior paint. Make sure you take note of any rotten siding, wood or brickwork that you may have to replace.

Electrical

Head to the electrical panel and meter. How old does it look? Are the fuses still functional and in use? Does it suit the present requirements of today, or does it require an update? Ensure you take note of the installation of high powered appliances like dryers and heaters if you need to. Likewise, consider the installation of HVAC equipment.

HVAC

Is there an HVAC system on the property? If yes, determine how old it looks and if it is still fully functional. Is the condenser and all other copper components still in place? Take a close look for things you must have missed, particularly in the internal equipment.

Interior Paint

There is a high possibility that you will need to repaint the interior of the home. Are there wallpapers to take out? Will you need to prime the walls? All of these will have an impact on your expenses later on.

Plumbing

Re-plumbing a property can cost you a huge amount of cash. Are the copper pipes still in place? Are there sinkholes in the front yard? Do you need to replace or upgrade the wall sinks or other fixtures? Outline the amount you will require for repairs later on.

Kitchen and Bath Remodel

Does the kitchen or bathroom look it is in great shape? If this is not the case, you may need to do some serious remodeling of these areas. Determine how this will fit in your budget and don't forget that a good looking bathroom and kitchen may help you sell your home faster.

Interior Floors

What sort of flooring was used in the home, do you

need to replace them? Will you require carpets? How much ceramic tile will you need?

Interior Fixtures

This can consist of items like doorknobs, light fixtures, ceiling fans, etc. These consist of all the little items that help in making a finished product look appealing. List down the things you need to add while taking a walk around the property.

Will you have to install a washer or refrigerator? How about a garbage disposal?

Chapter 6: Putting Your Team in Place

Having a great team in place for your rehab projects, especially if you are new to the venture, can help ensure the process goes as seamlessly as possible. In this chapter, we will be looking into some of the essential individuals you must have on your team. The first and most important team member is a general contractor.

General Contractor

Unless you are a licensed contractor yourself, you will require a general contractor and one you can depend on. An easy way to find a good contractor is to employ the help of search engines, but ensure you do not stop there. Some additional research can help you further streamline the options available to you.

Take a little time to do away with contractors with glaring red flags. These could be in the form of bad reviews from other investors or a bad rating from the BBB or Better Business Bureau. After these, you can further streamline your options by asking additional questions like the years of experience, similar jobs the contractor has handled, and so on. However, you need to ensure you choose the right contractor for your project as they can ensure everything goes as smoothly as it should.

Realtor

Realtors know where you can find real estate listings and new properties. You can find them with ease by running a search on the internet in your geographic location. Realtors can aid you in carrying out Comps on homes you want to purchase. Realtors are also vital in your marketing plan.

Real Estate Attorneys

There are a few investors who are of the notion that they can deal with the vast amount of documents and paperwork that come up during a rehab deal alone. This may be true for those with the required experience and qualifications. However, for many rehabbers, especially new rehabbers, getting a real estate attorney to go through the fine print can help you save a lot of headaches and time down the road.

When you sign a document you are unable to comprehend completely, the result is never a positive one. With lots of cash on the line, the implications could be devastating. Similar to having a real estate agent with the proper qualification to help you with the appropriate area to invest, collaborating with a lawyer who deals in real estate deals is also as crucial.

An Architect

With the right design for your renovation, you can sell your rehabbed property at the best price and fast. The appropriate architect will help you develop a design buyers will like in the form of a blueprint, which will consist of any structural changes and building material specifications your project will need.

The designs developed by the architect will be required to satisfy inspectors, get building permits, and make sure that contractors who place bids on your project are placing correct pricing and offering you precisely what you requested.

An Experienced Permit-Expeditor

One of the major challenges you will deal with as a rehabber, is getting the appropriate permits and obtaining project approval from inspectors. Regardless of where you are situated, you can make this process seamless by collaborating with a permit expeditor.

The leading permit expeditors are those who used to work at the inspection or local permit office till they retired and now consult with builders. These experts can help you cut off weeks from the inspection and permit process. Like we stated in earlier chapters, time is money when it comes to real estate, and the returns you get relate directly to how fast you can sell your rehab property.

A Skilled Stager

Stagers are usually featured on many house flipping shows, and this is not without reason. With the appropriate décor and furniture, a property's marketability can instantly be enhanced. Along with that, it can help you increase the price you sell your property for and reduce the time it takes to dispose of it. What's more, the right staging can help buyers see themselves living in the property, which can trigger quick sales, since buying decisions are usually made using emotion.

A Local Appraiser

As a rehabber, you need to understand what you need to pay presently (as-is value), and the amount you can sell a property for (after repair value) once you are through with your renovations. An appraiser can check out recent sales of properties similar to yours and help you estimate these values.

Your gross profit is the difference between both values, so it is vital to collaborate with an appraiser who can accurately attain this value.

Insurance Agent

Every rehab project needs builder's risk insurance, and an insurance agent with the proper qualifications can elaborate on the deductibles, exclusions, and limits for those coverages. Policy terms and coverages will differ based on the area the property is located, and it is vital to make sure you have coverage in the event of accidents that may take place on your job location. Not doing this may result in you spending money on legal fees and hospital bills in the event an accident occurs.

A Title and Settlement Company

Properties with title issues or complex ownership can be ideal to purchase because many people avoid dealing with these kinds of problems. However, if you have a settlement company agent with vast experience, who understands how to deal with those issues, you can capitalize on those opportunities without any competition.

Lenders

Lenders are also vital members of a great team. They will offer you the funds to buy and fix the property. Regardless of the kind of project you are taking up, at some point, you will want to determine the sort of financing you require.

Even experienced investors in real estate leverage on financing for a host of their deals. By doing this, they don't invest so much of their funds into a single project. By leveraging on the benefits of private funding, investors can spread their funds over multiple projects as opposed to a single project.

An Amazing Leader: You!

Similar to lots of great teams, your rehab team requires a team lead. This is the area you can step in. After you have put together the appropriate team members, all that is left for you is to urge them to put their best into your project. Ultimately, this will result in the highest level of success and returns for all parties involved.

Even with the right team in place, not managing your rehab to some extent will lead to a flop in your house flip. The subsequent chapter will show you how to manage your rehab property to make sure you get the best results.

Chapter 7: Managing Your Rehab

If you have made it this far, then it implies that you have set up most of the essentials. But that does not mean the job on your hands is complete. The truth is that even with the most reliable team members in place, it will still be vital for you to manage the project to make sure it all goes according to plan. When it has to do with projects, including rehab projects, learning proper management is essential.

Any single moment you waste towards the completion of your project means additional costs for you. This could range from labor costs and holding costs, among others. All of these added up could make a significant dent in your pockets.

Knowing all of these, you need to ensure you properly manage your projects. Below are some things that can be of help.

Develop the Scope of Work

Some general contractors have the capacity to deal with all areas of the project. But, a lot of them are unable to perform tasks like electrical or rewiring. Likewise, if you are getting the service of other vendors and subcontractors, you will need to outline their duties clearly. This means you need to deliberate on the individuals you will designate tasks to. The major thing here is to develop a plan which shows who is responsible for handling each task even before you start.

Develop a Back-up Plan

Even if you made all the right plans, there might be moments when issues that you did not plan for will arise, while your project is going on. To deal with situations like these, it is ideal that you have a plan B in place to deal with these sorts of issues, especially if the property is a very old one. Like we have covered in earlier chapters, you can never fully tell what you will find when working in old buildings.

When these forms of issues arise, having a backup plan can help you stay on the right path when problems come up. Ponder on the options available to you and decide on a course of action.

Pay Contractors Only After They Have Finished the Work

Lots of new investors make the error of paying the

complete sum even before the start of the project. This is never the right decision because many times, the contractor completes the work and absconds with the money mid-way into the project, leaving you stranded. For those that can get back their money, it is only possible after placing numerous calls to the contractor. However, the mistake would have already been made, and the project will take much longer than bargained for to complete.

To ensure you don't fall into this trap, ensure you pay contractors at milestones. For example, a particular percentage of money up-front before the project start, a little more after completing a set part of the task, and so on.

Make Yourself Physically Available

If you are collaborating with a reliable team which you have worked with previously, you may not need this. But if it will be impossible for you to be at the site all through the project, try to pay surprise visits once in a while. A lot of new rehabbers make the error of informing their contractors when they will be on the ground, which will make the contractor sit up towards the expected visit period. Make sure you pay surprise visits as this will help you learn if the contractor is focusing on your work during the period he should. It will also help you learn if there is progress being made on your task.

You can scramble the timing of your visits to the work site. If this is going to be a constraint for you, tell someone you can rely on to do this for you. This will ensure contractors don't slack and are ensuring they are doing all they can to complete your project fast.

Have a Relationship with Your Suppliers

There are home rehabbers who handle all aspects of the project, including materials. In contrast, there are house flippers who delegate all of these to their contractors, so they don't have to handle the stress involved. It is dependent on you to pick the one you are okay with.

But, you have to note that if given this task, contractors will go with less costly materials. This may not have an impact on little things, but for essential aspects of the home, you want the best. A better way of dealing with this would be to have a depot where you have a personal relationship. You can make an arrangement with them where they supply the materials you need when the moment comes, and let your contractor get the materials that are not as important.

Get The Services of an Expert

It can be rewarding to manage your project by

yourself. You learn new things and make sure your project goes the way it should and is completed within the set time. However, you will need some skills to get this done. You have to be organized, strategic, confident, and can handle the pressure. Likewise, it is vital for you to have ample time to monitor work progress, all of which may not be possible if you are always engaged in other tasks.

If you can afford it, you can get the services of a project manager to help you out. If you can get the best outcomes by channeling more resources as opposed to handling it on your own and be left with a shoddy job, then this is the way to go.

Chapter 8: Real Estate Dos and Don'ts

In the past, rehabbing homes was a fantastic way of investing in a project and getting huge returns. But now, it is not as easy as it used to be. Nonetheless, this does not imply that there is no avenue to make money from flipping homes. It only means that you have to exercise more caution when going about it. A great way of doing this is to learn the dos and don'ts of rehabbing homes to enable you to invest your money the right way and enhance your possibility of yielding good returns. In this chapter, we will be taking a look at some of the dos and don'ts of rehabbing, common mistakes, and tips to ensure you are successful in your rehab project. First, let's explore some of the dos and don'ts.

Do Understand What You Are Delving Into

Flipping homes is more complicated than it is portrayed to be on flipping shows. It requires a substantial investment at the start and extra costs as you go forward. Before you begin, you need to get yourself familiar with all the real estate rules and regulations in the areas you are in, so you will understand your restrictions and what you are allowed to do. There are things you may want to do on a property that will need you to get some permits which may sometimes be pricey. If you are prepared for the costs that may arise as you go forward, you can make allocations for them in your budget. Try to get in contact with a real estate attorney you can rely on to provide you with the best advice.

Don't Undermine the Issues That May Arise

The business of flipping homes is one with a lot of risks, and there are a lot of things that could go awry even before you list your property on the market. It is a good idea to make a proper plan; however, no amount of planning would prevent you from dealing with unforeseen circumstances as you go on. This is particularly the case with old buildings as you never can tell what you will find when you rip open a cabinet or wall. Problems with plumbing, obsolete wiring, mold, and a lot of other issues are some of the few unplanned issues you may be faced with.

Allocate some funds in your budget to cover these likely issues. As a rule of thumb, set aside 10 -20% of your entire budget for these surprises. There are times when this may be inadequate, but it will be enough to get you started.

See the Possibilities in a Fixer Upper

If you want to flip a home, going for a fixer-upper can be a great choice. Most times, you will be able to find good deals on properties that require updates or repairs. Make some upgrades, do these repairs and sell for a lot higher than the purchase price. Look at the structure of the property, is the layout great? Are the rooms wide enough? Is there anything unique buyers will want? If this is your first time doing a real estate rehab, go for properties that require the least amount of work.

Don't Overlook Huge Issues for a Reduced Price

Everyone wants a good deal when purchasing a property, and it can be refreshing to find a home for a low cost in good shape. However, don't buy a home because it has a low price while ignoring repairs that may cost you a fortune down the line. Some of the priciest projects to deal with in a home include:

- Bringing down walls

- Moving a kitchen or bathroom

- Stripping a kitchen or bathroom

- Changing structural walls

- Fixing issues with the foundation of a home

- Fixing roofs

- Changing the location of a chimney or fireplace

- Completing a basement that hasn't been completed

Indeed, you may find other issues along the way as you fix the property that may cost you a lot. But, these problems listed above are some of the costliest which you can see from your first visit to the home. A better option would be to go with your contractor when checking out the home for the first time. With his/her expertise, you will be able to learn about the kind of renovations you should be expecting on the property even before you begin.

Do Consider the Location

The neighborhood property is located in can have a lot of effects on how fast you sell it. However, homes in great neighborhoods may require some additional money. If you come across a property at a fantastic location for a low price, it means you may have to do a lot of work on the property. You may even have to deal with some major fixes. However, it may be worth the purchase, and you can determine this by checking out the comps in the area. Are other properties selling at a much higher range than the one you are currently trying to buy? If yes, this may be a very excellent investment. If the amount you will spend on purchasing the home and doing renovations is still not above the selling price of other homes in the area, then you can make high returns. It is particularly true if there are no issues with the core areas of the home like the kitchen, bathrooms, and sitting room, among others.

Location can also be harmful too. You may come across a fantastic property that requires just a little repair in a lousy area. You may also locate a great property that is not close to excellent roads or facilities. It is vital to consider these things because you will find it more challenging to sell a property that is not in a great location. Ensure you do your research on all the environmental factors that may prevent buyers from purchasing the property like airports, busy roads, and train tracks, among others.

Don't Ignore Landscaping and Curb Appeal

If you make the interior of the home amazing and ignore the exterior completely, your potential customer may not even give the home a second glance, nor walking in to check out the interior. It won't be easy to sell your property for the actual value if you don't put in the needed time to make the exterior appealing.

Reach out to a landscaper for ideas and work in line with your budget. A few touches of appeal to the exterior of your property can allow you to sell at a premium price.

Do Try Foreclosed Properties

If you go the direction of purchasing properties that have been foreclosed, it may be a great idea to go with post-foreclosure real estate and do your research on the home title before you purchase the property. When you purchase a property at a real estate auction, you may have to deal with a few liens, back taxes, and pending mortgage payments. All of these can dive into your budget. It is also vital to note that the majority of the foreclosed properties are sold as is, which implies that you may have to do most of the repairs on both the property and the home itself. Nonetheless, checking out a foreclosure may give you access to some fantastic deals.

Don't Let Yourself be Taken Aback

Rehabbing properties is an activity that comes with a lot of stress. However, if you make a proper budget, plan your time, and work with reliable team members, the process should go as smoothly as possible. However, if you are not sure if rehabbing homes is what you want to do, stay away from it. It is a massive responsibility and is not one that you should take lightly. If the project looks like it's going beyond what you can deal with, take a few steps back and relax. Weigh all the options available to you and pick the best route to take.

Deal with the most significant tasks first, which include those things you have to do to make the home buyable. If there is not much left in your budget to do the less important things, you can still rest assured that you have dealt with the major aspects and will still be able to get a profit. You need to ensure you don't use sentiments here. You won't become a millionaire overnight by flipping homes, but if you are great at it and remain consistent, eventually you may start to bring in profit as time goes on.

The experience you get on the way will help you determine things that work and things that don't. You will pick up lessons from the mistakes you make and make adjustments in your next flip to ensure it does not happen again. You won't be successful from every flip, and you need to be ready for losses once in a while. If you feel you can't handle this, then flipping houses may not be ideal for you.

Don't Forgo Quality During the Rehab Process

While rehabbing a home, ensure you do it without cutting corners. Covering bad structures with a layer of paint does not make a home ready for flipping. The agent of your buyer will always be in search of signs like these. Even if you are doing the work by yourself, put in the effort to ensure you provide a quality result. The same applies if you outsource the job. Ensure you are working alongside professionals who take pride in what they do. Change those rusty fixtures in the bathroom or kitchen, take down that leaking cabinet and put up another, and fix electrical wiring if need be. The bottom line is; you need to repair things to get the best returns for your property. Do a job you indeed will be proud of.

Don't Go with Ancient Upgrades

When it has to do with making recent upgrades, go beyond your bathrooms and kitchens. It is not necessary to take down any fixture or part of the home that seems extremely old. However, you need to learn to differentiate from things that make the house appealing and those that give it an antique and unwelcoming look. To be on the safe side, its best to choose vintage items over those that are presently trending. The reason is that trends may change, but classics never change.

Major House Flipping Mistakes and How to Avoid Them

House flipping is a profitable venture if done the right way. However, making good returns is not as easy as it seems, especially as a first timer. There are lots of mistakes you could make, which is understandable due to the level of excitement that comes with the execution of a rehab project.

In this section, we will be looking into a few of the major flipping mistakes and how to avoid them.

Buying Excessively High

For many investors, the first location they check when they want to begin flipping is the market. However, the properties listed here are by agents who are on the MLS and list at market prices.

Due to the lack of knowledge of where to find excellent properties, lots of new flippers purchase any property that comes their way, with the hopes that the market will continue to go up. However, this is a setup for failure because as an investor, your goal should be to purchase a property that will bring you profit after you have deducted all the costs, including renovation costs.

Do not let the excitement get to you and lead you

into purchasing a property that has a very high price tag attached. Do your research like we have covered in earlier chapters to find the best deal available.

Believing That the Cheapest is the Best Option

Properties that are in terrible shape are the easiest to buy because of the low price tag associated with them. Sadly, these kinds of properties often require the most repairs and the highest level of experience to complete.

New investors who do not understand what a rehab entails or proper strategies to make the right estimate may not be able to determine the amount of work associated with fixing properties like these. Due to the factors above, they can't accurately project the rehab costs. The incompetence to plan for as much rehab costs as possible has an impact on the timeline for completing the flip, which in turn drags on the budget of the project.

Lastly, these kinds of projects have a considerable amount of risks attached to them, which new rehabbers may not have the capacity to deal with before they occur. For this reason, they continuously have to be on edge to correct issues, which result in more time and money.

In essence, because a property comes with a low price, does not imply you are getting a great deal.

Going in Way Over Your Head

There are lots of risks that come with rehabbing properties. However, the severity of these risks have been toned down by many recognized flipping shows on television. So, if you have not correctly done your research, then you may not be ready to deal with those risks.

If you are a new investor, you are sure to pay for inadequate knowledge with your money or time. The combination of this truth, with the purchase of a challenging rehab project like that stated above, can lead to a massive amount of losses for new investors.

To avoid this issue, you need to never underestimate how much knowledge you don't have. A better strategy when starting to flip homes is, to begin with a flip which is small and not as profitable. Doing this will help you understand the process and develop a dependable team to aid you with more considerable risks later on. You will learn on the move and make mistakes. However, if you keep learning and adapting, you will be well on your way to becoming better in the business of rehabbing homes.

Overspending for Assistance

When you have a reliable team of professionals backing you up all through the rehab process, you can capitalize on good pricing from them in return for continuous business from you. Realtors and contractors are also included in this team.

If you have no team available, and your contractor works with you like a typical client, you may need to pay premium prices. You need to locate a contractor that will collaborate with you for the lowest possible price without letting go of quality. The same also applies if you go with any realtor without negotiating the price. You will end up spending too much when selling your rehab home.

To ensure you don't pay too much for contractors to become a part of your team, you can begin by checking out websites like HomeAdvisor or Angie's List, but make sure you find out if the contractor is investor-friendly. With this, you will be able to screen those that have chosen to work alongside retail clients.

You can also look into local real estate investment clubs and request recommendations from other investors for a rehab friendly contractor. However, note that many of them may not be willing to part with this information.

Spending a Lot on Materials

Working alongside contractors who are investor-friendly is a great way to save funds on a real estate rehab. They understand that to flip a home, it is essential to reduce the cost of materials as much as possible. So, for instance, if a client requires a custom paint for their structure which is pricey, an investor-friendly contractor can combine some neutral paints to get the required color to save funds on paint and ensure that lots of people find the home appealing.

Even though lots of contractors do not head to large stores to buy materials, there are some ways to save funds on materials. This could range from purchasing materials in bulk, heading directly to a local distributor for volume discounts, or buying clearance items.

To ensure you don't pay excessively for materials, ensure you don't get too emotionally involved with finishes or materials. The property is not yours to live in but for your buyers. As you start to develop personal relationships with distributors and utilize some of the other techniques to purchase items, you may be able to ensure you avoid buying materials from contractors entirely and only reach out to them for labor. This way, you will be able to take full charge of the rehab process, and also avert the additional cost included by contractors.

Making Too Many Improvements

For many new home buyers, transforming a property which was once unappealing into one people will envy is the best part of the project. In the end, this results in excessive improvements to suit the current trends of the market.

This is not necessarily a bad thing for typical homeowners. However, for investors rehabbing a home, this is not a great idea. The goal of rehabbing a home is to turn it into something people would want to purchase at the best price. There will always be pressure between the demands of the market and what can be offered profitably. But lots of new rehabbers do not know the level of enhancement they require to be successful.

To avert improving a rehab property excessively, it is vital to learn how to locate accurate comps. If you can find the comps of remodeled homes in the same area, you will be able to project the level of enhancement you require to transform your rehab project to a level that will meet the expectations of buyers.

Another way of preventing over enhancement is to check out houses that have not been completed yet to find out if there are enhancements you can alter to reduce cost.

Spending Too Much Time

Taking up more than you can handle, engaging the wrong team and making too many improvements along with many of the other mistakes listed above can lead to an investor taking more time to flip a property than projected.

This form of long holding time can have massive adverse financial penalties, especially if the flip is funded with a Hard Money loan. This is because you will be charged massive amounts of cash for each day the flip goes beyond the stipulated date of completion.

To make sure you don't take too long, you need to have a comprehensive understanding of all the costs that come with a flip, so it becomes apparent when a deal is not worth the stress. This will become less difficult with every flip you come across. Ensure you carefully develop your team, check out licenses, references, and history.

Put a timeline for your construction in place and ensure you monitor the progress of your contractors continuously. Along with that, develop contacts that offer rewards for fast completion and penalizing lateness in project completion.

Not Having Adequate Cash

As we have previously covered, this is the major mistake many new investors make when they want to rehab a home. Before you begin, it is vital that you understand the amount of cash you require to complete a flip and ensure that you have the cash to cover the entire cost of all projects. Put simply, the profit you earn is dependent on appropriate cost planning and budgeting, which can aid you in making your project a success.

Not Putting a Business Plan in Place

Similar to any other business venture you are taking up, you need to outline a business plan for your rehab venture. By putting a plan in place before you delve in, it can also ensure you correctly understand the rewards and risks that are associated with successfully flipping a home.

Time is vital, especially when it comes to flipping properties, and wasting time can cost you cash. Having a business plan in place in addition to helping you estimate the possible costs and timeline you need for a project, can also ensure you know the rewards, ROI, and risks associated with a specific project. The longer it takes you to complete the project, the more your expenses in terms of utilities and property taxes, among others. With a comprehensive business plan in place, you will be able to note these costs and have a comprehensive overview of the whole project.

Not Buying Insurance

Failing to purchase property insurance before you invest in any property is a mistake made by many new investors. Property insurance refunds homeowners and minimizes the dangers for rehab projects if there are damages to the property like those caused by fire, theft, or flood.

If flipping properties has to do with getting a profit on your investment, then you want to ensure you keep all the resources and efforts you have channeled in the project secure. You can either buy property insurance coverage online or locally. However, it is a smart decision to compare prices for the best deal from more than one source as premiums differ.

Collaborating with the Wrong Partner

House flipping is a venture that comes with its hassles, so you want to collaborate with reliable sources and professionals who understand the process of rehab and have the capacity to take projects on. This means you need someone proficient and not a handyman you are close to because if the project does not go the way you plan, it can dent your relationship. It is not wise to dent your relationship over investments.

In contrast, when you work with a reputable plumber, or contractor that you have appropriately vetted, make sure the work you get is of high quality, which has a direct link to the profit you get. If you have unique property, like a classic one, it is ideal to collaborate with a professional who is skilled in these kinds of houses. A new home developer who is used to new properties may not understand the intricacies that come with a classic home. Always locate a reliable realtor, reach out to professionals that you have properly vetted, and develop a vast network of contractors with good standing in your neighborhood.

Failing to Understand Your Market

Similar to failing to collaborate with the right partners, not having a complete understanding of your market can put your investment at risk of failure. By carrying out a market analysis, you will be able to understand the rewards and risks in the area you choose, and it is crucial to selling your rehabbed home successfully.

It also ensures you can determine the best period for a home rehab in your neighborhood, and the present market trends in the area like the expected sale cost, housing demand and what home buyers like among many others. With a market analysis alongside a business plan, you will be able to better prepare for the entire rehab process alongside any other thing that come up later.

Not Putting Up an Exit Strategy

Finally, to make sure you are successful in the venture of flipping homes, you need to always have an exit strategy in place which is heavily dependent on the price you have placed on the home. Communicate with your realtor to help you with the right price, which will help you sell your home fast, and reduce the carrying costs you incur. Every good thing requires time and becoming successful at flipping homes is not something that takes place in one night. It is an investment that requires skill, research, preparation, and a great team.

Lots of newbies to investing are often in a hurry to complete their first deal and rush into anyone that comes their way without considering the negative aspects of a flip. To be very successful, familiarize yourself with the dos and don'ts and ensure you don't make any of the mistakes during your first flip. With time, you will become highly successful in the business.   Now that you understand the mistakes you should not make, we will be looking into a few factors that can have an impact on your rehab in the next chapter.

Chapter 9: Risk Factors That Impact Rehab

The market for real estate is affected by a range of factors beyond human control. As many investors in real estate know, it is not possible to project or control it completely. These numerous factors have an impact on how you would purchase and sell your rehab property. In this chapter, we will be looking into a few of the common factors that can have an impact on your rehab property.

Micro-Factors That Have an Effect on Rehab homes

The Location of the Property

You may have come across the term location at some point; however, when it has to do with the prices of properties or your home rehab, it has to do with some crucial factors that have an impact on the buyer's lifestyle in general which include:

- The quality of schools around which is a vital factor for lots of buyers who have kids still in school

- For buyers at employment age, closeness to opportunities for employment is a major priority

- For younger buyers, closeness to recreational facilities and shopping centers is of high value. However, it will affect the prices for every home buyer.

All of these factors work alongside each other and all preferences that can affect your rehab in terms of pricing. Likewise, note that if you are getting a property which has two of these three features, you should be ready to pay premium prices and deal with a lot of competition for the property. If you are after a property that has all these features, then you should have a huge amount of financial backing.

Upgrades and Updates

Lots of buyers prefer homes that have been recently updated and upgraded with the most recent fittings. As stated by the National Association of Realtors, upgraded bathrooms and kitchens are one of the most vital upgrades buyers are after and can result in a lot of stress if the buyer has to upgrade them on their own. In essence, the kind of upgrades you make on a rehab property can have a considerable impact on your overall profit.

Inspection Report

The inspection report can have a significant impact on the price of your rehab property. When you are through with your rehab, and the buyer still finds hidden issues in your property, the higher the room for negotiation they have. If the deal does not go through with this buyer, you as the seller are liable to reveal the inspection report to buyers in the future, which further reduces the chances of selling at the price originally listed.

Neighborhood Comps

Comps or Comparable properties sold in your neighborhood have an impact on the value of your rehab property. Real estate agents as well as appraisers analyze homes that have features similar to yours and use it as a yardstick against the potential price of your home. The more the value of properties similar to yours, the higher you can sell and vice versa.

Macro-Factors That Have an Impact on Rehab

Economic Indicators

There is a range of factors in the economy that can have an effect on the housing market. The state economy, national economy, and local economy are linked but can slightly differ based on the location. Consumer confidence and political climate also affect the economy, and it is difficult to measure these things precisely. As stated by reports, there were over 200,000 jobs added in addition to enhanced economic recovery. These kinds of numbers can aid individuals in predicting the coming trends in real estate.

How strong the economy is also generally has a significant impact on the market for real estate. This is because the capacity of customers to afford the prices of houses is dependent on vital factors like income growth, unemployment as well as GDP. During the Great Recession, which took place from 2008 - 2012, the link between real estate and the economy as a whole was revealed. Local economies which had a huge number of jobs related to real estate, be it in mortgage financing or construction, experienced a drastic depreciation in the prices of properties.

Nature

An excellent example of this is Houston. More than 160,000 houses were destroyed by Hurricane Harvey in less than a week. It took around 90 hours to change the previously prosperous real estate market. Neighborhoods formerly filled with life were transformed to dead zones, and homeowners began to rent out their homes instead, while individuals who were displaced from their homes went about in search of a fast solution to their diverse circumstances.

Nature can have a tremendous effect on the market of real estate, and it comes without any prior notice. In 2017, after the storm, the market was left in a strange shape. Aside from the walls that vanished, and the properties that were wrecked, the listings on the market increased while the sales prices were lower. In a year, things in the market began to become normal. The return to normalcy to the market began to push it back towards a seller's market. In a place like Harris County, even though the prices of homes were double digits before it was hit by the hurricane, there has only been a 2 percent increase. However, a report comparing those that wanted to leave and those who wanted to move in and remain, the latter had a higher value.

Simultaneously, the impact of the storm has

changed the housing trends. Individuals in specific areas in Houston have started to construct their houses ten feet above the ground. Likewise, flipping houses has become a great way to make money for smart investors. A lot of them ran to the damages homes and purchased them for a fraction of what they cost before the hurricane. They made efforts to rehab them, sell them, and put them up for rent.

Interest Rates

The "Fed interest rate" is another factor that can affect your rehab. This rate is a very crucial factor in determining how mortgage rates are created because it determines the cost for banks to loan cash. When there is a low fed interest rate, it means less mortgage rates offered by banks, which in turn reduces the homebuyer's monthly mortgage payments for a specific mortgage amount.

The less the payment that needs to be made monthly, the more affordable prospective buyers find a loan. This reality can enhance the size of mortgage homebuyers can get, which may enhance the prices of properties. You need to run your numbers before you purchase homes to determine the interest rate as it can either make your property affordable or unaffordable to prospective buyers.

Investors

The housing crisis brought about a market which was appealing to investors who had an interest in residential real estate. The rise in the number of short sales and foreclosures gave both foreign and domestic investors the chance to clinch cheap properties either to sell for profit or rehab. A research done by the National Association of Realtors proved that the amount of homes investment buyers purchased on the market stood at around 20 percent. In essence, as the number of distressed homes begins to go down, the market may slow down as soon as these investors reduce their purchases. At some point, if not timed correctly, a lot of these investors may want to let go of their properties at the same time, which may lead to a lot of homes being listed on the market at the same time. This could have an impact on how much you buy or sell your rehab property.

Other Factors

Period of the Year

Houses are sold all year round. However, there is a noticeable pattern to it. Typically, sales become low in the later parts of January and February and get to a peak around July. You need to understand when your project will be ready for listing on the market. If you complete a rehab and place the home in January, you may spend more time on the market as opposed to if you listed it in July. You may also need to offer more affordable pricing to get ahead.

Valuation

When evaluating a possible deal, the most vital part of it is determining what the ARV or after repair value will be. If you don't make your purchase offer based on the results you get from your calculation, it will have a huge impact on the profit you make from your rehab property. You may end paying too excessively and be left with no profit.

You can also get the help of an experienced broker to help you determine your ARV, especially one who is active in the market your property is in. If you don't want this option, you can instead hire an appraiser to help you carry out an ARV appraisal using your rehab plans. If you are uncertain, get ideas from numerous valuations, because if you purchase a property at the wrong price, your possibility of making cash reduces drastically.

Experience and Capacity of Investor

Your experience will have a lot of impact on how

successful your first home rehab will be. If you have no experience and don't seek help from someone more skilled, you may end up at a loss. A better way would be to get the help of someone more proficient for a start while you develop your experience with time. Having a good team behind you can be of help at this point.

Your abilities are somewhat related to your experience. There are projects you will take on which won't align with the skill set you have. Perhaps you are more comfortable updating new structures and have no idea of how to bring out the best results in old structures. If you don't have a reliable team behind you, or someone to show you the ropes, its best to stick to deals within your skill set for the best results.

Renovation Budget

The budget you have put in place for renovation should be a huge factor in the initial purchase price. If you forget to do this, you may not make a profit, even if you do all other aspects the right way.

Ensure you have inspected and addressed everything you can see, and remember to renovate for your buyer and not yourself. Rather, focus on:

- Fixing all items that have been damaged

- Updating out of date fixtures. Keeping these in mind can have a lot of impact on how your first property rehab deal goes.

- Hidden Repairs

You will find them in almost all homes. You may rip down a kitchen cabinet to meet lots of other structural issues. Or maybe you find out the roof is weak after you have purchased the property. Whether you find issues like these can impact your property rehab positively or negatively depending on what you find.

Issues with Contractors

This is also another crucial factor that can determine if your real estate rehab deal fails or succeeds. If you pick the wrong contractor for your job, you have automatically set yourself up to fail. To sort this issue, your best bet is to weed out the contractors who don't have the skills for your project with a comprehensive vetting process.

Ensure you have a very detailed contract, which covers everything that has to do with the task at hand. Plan for anything that might go wrong in the contract, so you can refer to it in the event of a disagreement. When it is certain that the contractor is refusing to make amends, do not hesitate to let him go and move on. With a comprehensive vetting process and an elaborate contract, you can get rid of most issues you will deal with in this area.

Change in Demographics

All generations come with their traits. For instance, it has been observed that the generation of millennials would rather rent as opposed to buy. However, recent data shows that in recent times, Millennials are actually purchasing more houses, and may have just held on for a little longer. Likewise, changing population patterns in areas like cultural differences, age, and gender can have an impact on how you should approach the market and have a lot of influence on your next rehab deal.

Chapter 10: Outsourcing or Doing it Yourself?

Another vital aspect of flipping a home is to determine what aspects to outsource and which to do on your own. Engaging in areas you can't handle on your own can lead to a massive loss of cash in the long run. However, outsourcing basic things you could have done on your own could lead to a rise in expenses. For this reason, there needs to be a balance when it comes to doing this. In this chapter, we will explore how you can effectively determine what parts to do on your own and those areas to outsource to a professional.

Outsourcing to a General Contractor – Why Should You?

When you have an experienced general contractor in your house flipping team, they can provide you with a lot of help in organizing your project and offering insights into things you can do in a property.

A general contractor can keep your project going

when you are not there and ensure the work is completed within the set time. You can charge the contractor with the task of getting you the permits you need and letting you know how long each process for getting permits will last. Hiring contractors can be pricey, but the benefits you gain at the end will be worth it.

When you use a contractor, it will be more expensive than if you handled the project on your own. However, it will help you save money and time during the length of a project. A contractor can act as a manager on your site, who stays full time, and the implication of this is reduction of waste on the site in addition to a quick completion of the project. In essence, if you outsource some of these areas to your contractor, it will help you cut down on cost and also increase the profit you make on a rehab property.

Doing it Yourself

Like we have earlier stated, doing the rehab project on your own can help you reduce expenses. So, if you have the time and skills to engage in the rehab project on your own, then it is a way to go. Many investors do their rehab by themselves, but if you don't have the needed level of experience to do the work, this may not be the best route for you.

Even if you possess the needed skills, the following are some questions you need to answer before you proceed:

- Do you like doing physical work?

- Do you complete tasks you begin?

- Are your skill levels where they need to be?

- Do you have adequate time?

- Do you understand where permits will be required, and how to get them?

- Do you know the local building codes?

- Do you have the financial resources to deal with this kind of project?

- Do you have the resources in terms of finance and time to complete the project?

If your answer to any of the questions above is "NO" then you may need to reconsider if doing the work on your own is the best step. You need to be honest when evaluating your level of skills, money, and time. So having learned the implications of both, what areas should you outsource and which should you not?

Areas to Outsource and What Not to

Now, the first question you need to answer here is: *what is the reason for doing the work on your own?*

There are two major reasons why investors choose to do the work themselves. The first is to save cost, and the other is the joy being physically involved in what a flip offers them.

However, you need to exercise caution if your reason is to save cost because, in the end, you may spend more if you take up the tasks by yourself. It may even lead to more time on the project because if you don't do it properly, you may have to do it all over again. Sometimes, even before you restart the project, the wrong work you did initially may have caused some new problems for your rehab, which will require even more time to fix.

You may want to engage in some of the work on your own, but it's best not to do all. The least complicated way to determine the tasks you can complete and those that you can't is to classify them.

The first group could be the basic tasks

- **Basic Tasks**: This will consist of things that

are easy to do, like cleaning, painting, demolition, installing new sinks, and faucets, among many others. It should include things that you are aware have the least possibility of making matters worse. These kinds of tasks are not tricky, and if you have the time, it will probably be a great idea to do them on your own. They are an excellent method of saving resources if your goal is to earn a profit from your home rehab.

The next group could be the complex tasks

- **Complex Tasks**: This will include tasks that are a bit more complex. Here, include tasks that you will need to utilize power tools and electrical equipment. This could include fixing holes in walls or fixing tiles.

The last are the advanced tasks

- **Advanced Tasks**: Here, you will include the most complex projects. The tasks here will need a high level of experience and could consist of re-plumbing or rewiring a home. It could also consist of making changes to the structure of the home. The tasks here are perhaps the ones you would want to outsource to professionals who specialize in these sorts of tasks. These kinds of tasks may need professionals who have a license that allows them to do the work in the first place. By taking up tasks like these on your own, you may be leaving yourself open to legal issues down the road.

Determining all of these can take a lot of time, but taking the wrong step can wreck your entire project. However, before choosing the professionals to outsource parts of your project to, make sure you do a comprehensive vetting process so you can get the best hands for your project. Hiring wrong hands can have the same negative implications as doing tasks yourself without experience.

Coupled with hiring these professionals with an elaborate vetting system, you need to make yourself available to monitor what they are doing or at least provide solutions to problems that may arise during the project.

In essence, you can save cash if you do some parts of the projects on your own as opposed to outsourcing. However, if you don't have the necessary expertise, you may end up causing havoc to your project. You need to have proper knowledge of the tasks that you need to outsource and those that you should take up.

Chapter 11: Which Are the Most Important Skills to Have?

Purchasing a home, rehabbing it and selling it fast for profit is not a strategy that is possible without preparation. It needs finance, perseverance when hindrances come up and more importantly, some vital skills to help you along the way. Sadly, individuals who see lots of shows about flipping houses on TV believe it is an easy method of getting rich without any form of preparation or skills. The belief that house flipping is easy could not be any further from the truth, and it is a route that is almost certain to lead you to failure.

If you plan on being a successful flipper, you will have to develop specific skills in addition to keeping reliable professionals close to you. In this chapter, we will be taking a look at some of the vital skills you need to develop if you want to be successful in the business of rehabbing.

Negotiation Skills

If you want to maximize the profit on your investment, it is vital to master the art of negotiation. The rehab process has to do with a lot of negotiation at almost every step. First, you will need to negotiate when buying the property, you want to flip. Next, you negotiate with contractors when they bring in their bids for the projects. Lastly, you will negotiate with buyers who have an interest in your rehab property. Regardless of where you find yourself, you can enhance your skills in negotiation using the following:

- Do your research: Ensure that you do the numbers many times. Determine the peak amounts you can spend while ensuring you don't exceed your budget and still make a profit. In addition, make efforts to know the present state of any property you want to purchase alongside the neighborhood comp details. There are repair requirements that can offer you a fantastic position for negotiating a better offer.

- Maintain your stand: Don't falter with your budget and numbers. If the seller does not agree with your best price, feel free to walk away. It's best to walk away from a property that won't yield any returns instead of investing cash you won't get back from it.

- Take advantage of silence: Awkward silences can do you a lot of good when it comes to negotiations. Most times, a seller will be eager to get rid of the tension by agreeing with your terms.

Marketing Skills

To sell a rehab property for profit, you need to be well skilled in marketing. You need to learn how to promote the property, stage the property, hire amazing realtors, and host open houses. However, your skills in marketing won't apply to just the selling process. You need these skills to find the ideal property for your needs. Below are a few ways you can use your skills in marketing to find the right home to flip:

- Leverage flyers: Get out the word that you are in search of properties to purchase using flyers. If it is allowed, you can also take advantage of signposts.

- Use social media: Take advantage of your social media platforms like Pinterest, Facebook, Twitter, and Instagram, among others, about your willingness to purchase properties.

Painting skills

You can save yourself lots of expenses by developing a skill like painting. By doing the interior painting of your home, you can save a lot of expenses going forward. There are numerous how-to videos and tips online, which can teach you how to do a good paint job.

Ability to Evaluate Properties

This is a very vital skill which is not easy to develop. You need to have the capacity to determine homes in poor condition and also conclude what the value will be when you are through renovating it. After repair value in addition to the transaction costs, improvement costs, cost of financing, and profit are all vital figures that will help you learn the amount you should pay for a property.

When beginning, you need to get the help of experienced flippers and realtors to help you develop this skill. Another way is to check out a real estate website which shows the prices of homes in areas you have an interest in. Make a comparison of the prices and facilities all the properties that have been sold have and try to determine the facilities that offer more value. Next, search for properties on sale in the area and try to project the selling price. After these houses have been sold, check out the selling price to find out if you were correct or close. Likewise, there are lots of books you can read that will help you develop this skill.

Estimating Costs of Construction

In the absence of this, you will be unable to create the right budget for the home renovations, which will be crucial for the completion of any flip. You can hire contractors to assist you here; however, you still need to have a knowledge of the cost of installing plumbing, wiring, flooring, decking, and cabinets, among others. To help you out here, you can get estimates from experienced contractors and take advantage of software applications.

Financial Skills

You don't need to be as skilled as an accountant, but you should have the capacity to put together all the various costs and estimates that will let you know how much you need to purchase a property and get returns. In addition, since you may be sourcing for finance, you need to understand how it works in terms of interest and others. Lastly, you may need to learn how to use accounting software or spreadsheets to keep a properly updated record of expenses. All of these can be delegated to a CPA who you could hire later on, but for a start, it is a vital skill you need to learn.

Dealing with Contractors

If you don't learn how to communicate with

contractors respectfully, pay them when it is due, request that they do not compromise the quality of work, and finish up at the agreed date, then you may fail even before you start. It is best to always have a contract in writing which shows all that should be completed and the terms for payment. Generally, you need to be fair while remaining tough, which can be a very difficult thing to learn as a starter. You can check out investment forums on real estate to get further help in developing this skill.

Knowing Which Parts to Outsource

It will be impossible to learn all the skills you need. Even if you can, you may not have the resources and time to develop them to the highest level. For this reason, you need to be able to decide which areas you will outsource and which to do yourself. This is vital if you want to flip homes successfully and fast.

If you try to do everything on your own, the process will only slow down, and it may hurt your business. Perhaps you are very skilled at marketing but know nothing about construction? Then get a professional contractor to handle that area while you focus on what you are great at.

How to Choose Appropriate Tools

You need the skill of determining the facilities prospective buyers would love. A trending faucet? A smart home? A larger kitchen with white countertops? You need to have the skills to determine the enhancements that will be right for a specific property. You can't choose the same enhancements for a $600k home and a $150k home. If you spend too much on improving a home that is not worth it, you may not make returns when you finally sell off the property. You can get advice from other more experienced experts in the field while you develop your skill in this area further.

Basic Construction Skills

Skills in construction are vital for a range of reasons. For instance, if you are skilled at painting, plumbing, or wiring electricity, you can do the work by yourself to ensure the renovation is completed fast. In another instance, your knowledge in any of these fields will help you evaluate what your contractors have done. It will ensure it is more difficult for any of these contractors to take advantage of you. More importantly, you don't need to have in-depth knowledge to determine if a job has been carried out appropriately. To develop this skill, you can talk to other experts or read books to educate yourself. You can also check out finished jobs and read posts about your desired skill.

Design and Decorating Skills

When rehabbing a home or property, you will need to make choices regarding decoration. There are choices to be made concerning light fixtures, flooring, and many others, which will have a huge impact on the interest of buyers in the property. To develop your skills in these areas, you can go through magazines, see popular house flipping shows or go to as many house showings as you can for ideas.

Knowledge of Where to Find Contractors and Materials

It is essential to develop an elaborate knowledge of where to get building materials to ensure you only get top prices and have sources to fall back on when required. Having sources close by can ensure products are delivered to your project site quickly when work is ongoing, in the event of an emergency.

In addition, you need to have a list of contractors in place, who can help in achieving your objectives. It is vital to have a list of many contractors in place, so if one is occupied with other jobs, you can seek the help of another. On top of that, you can capitalize on specific contractors for specific kinds of jobs. For instance, if you have a small renovation, you could handle it on your own, or have a specific contractor for the job. You could also have another contractor who you will task with a large rehab project.

Computer Skills

Real estate investment is starting to have more ground online. You check out properties online and also communicate with realtors, contractors, and other vital individuals online through emails and other platforms.

In addition, there are software applications used to keep records of your financing and evaluate deals. This means you require basic computer skills to effectively do all of these. There are a ton of books and tutorials on the internet that can help you out with developing this skill.

Project Management Skills

To rehab a home the right way, you need to plan properly and maintain a schedule. It requires that you communicate with every party involved in fixing the home. If you want to be a successful rehabber, you may never pick up a tool to do any construction; however, it is vital for you to learn how to properly manage a project the right way.

Problem Solving Skills

As a home rehabber, you are likely to come across hidden issues the instant you begin to break down floors and walls. The capacity to evaluate these issues and think about a solution on the spot will make sure that the project continues to go on fast.

Relationship Management Skills

As a real estate investor, you will be working alongside and managing a lot of relationships. This could include relationships with contractors, inspectors, government agencies, buyers, and so on. By learning to connect with individuals the right way and develop positive relationships, your rehab process will go more seamlessly.

The Capacity to Finish the Right Way

When beginning a property rehab, it is not difficult to foresee the rehab in different strokes when large changes have to be carried out . However, finishing with details is a different skill-set. The capacity to envision the larger picture and follow up with the needed details is quite vital, particularly if you plan to get the best price for your property.

Rehabbing a home is an amazing method of investing cash, but not everyone can be successful in doing it. However, if you can master the skills we have discussed above, you are well on your way to being a successful rehabber.

Chapter 12: The Closing Process

If you have not sold or purchased a home before, this process can be a scary one. In addition to getting the appropriate timing, there are numerous things you need to do for the transaction to be successful. If you are collaborating with an agent, it may be less difficult, but it is ideal for you to learn how to get the best deal possible and complete the sale fast. All of these will ensure you don't waste time and cash during the process. All of these are what we will be looking into in the subsequent pages.

What is Closing?

This is when the buyer and seller of a home gratify all the promises proposed in the sales contract. Typically, it has to do with the transfer of cash and documents, so that the seller, which is you, can transfer ownership and control of the home to the buyers. Then, you will pay all the loans left on the property and pay all of the individuals who aided in ensuring the sales and closing went through.

Now, let's look into what the closing process

includes for you as the home seller.

House Closing Process

Negotiating

When an offer is made on your home by a buyer, there are three routes you can take:

- Accept the contract terms

- Make a counteroffer and change some of the terms

- Reject the offer and walk away

You have to make efforts to learn the motivation for a buyer wanting to buy your property. Knowing this will help you negotiate terms which are more favorable to you in addition to the price. You can make them cover precise repairs which may be uncovered during an inspection, or settle fees that would normally be yours to pay.

You also need to keep your emotions in check while negotiating. The transaction is not personal, and you want to keep it at just business. You want to make sure your buyer stays happy as you may still need him/her for a few other things before closing the sale. If you have many offers, you can use that to your advantage. Let the competing buyers be aware that someone else is offering a higher price and give them the chance to change their prices. Set up a date and time when you will choose the top offers. Any buyer who has a genuine interest in the home you are selling will be quick in providing feedback.

Push the negotiations for as long as you want, but remember not to overdo it. Your goal is to sell your property as fast as you can for profit, which means you don't want to drag the process excessively. This part of the closing process should take three days or less, or the buyer may no longer have an interest in your property.

Closing

During the closing process, the buyer and seller have to be present, with their lawyers if necessary, real estate agents, as well as closing agents. If you aren't going along with your lawyer, get your closing documents in advance. If you are closing for the first time, study all of the closing documents with your attorney, to enable you to have an understanding of what you want to append your signature to.

After signing every document, you are through with the closing process. Make sure the money you are getting aligns with what you are supposed to get on the disbursement sheet. If it does not tally, make certain it does before leaving. The disbursement sheet is a legal record of the transaction, so it needs to be correct.

The title agency you are collaborating with will have already gone through the title history of the property and if everything goes well, they will have sorted out all the remaining problems with the title. The title agency will have the responsibility of making sure the figures tally, issuing checks, and putting together all the signatures and ensuring they are valid.

The closing process can be time-consuming for you if you don't get things ready in advance. However, if you prepare in advance, the experience will be less stressful for everyone involved.

Chapter 13: Wealth Growing and Investment Strategies

As a property rehabber, taxes can take a huge chunk of your profit. For this reason, you need to arm yourself with wealth building and retirement strategies, which will ensure you can keep more of the money you make from flipping homes and increase your earnings. Below are two major strategies.

Using the 1031 Exchange

The 1031 exchange is a tool that gives real estate investors, including rehabbers the chance to function with reduced involvement from the IRS. In turn, this reduces a huge amount of tax costs going forward.

But, there are a few guidelines that define the kind of property that is eligible for a 1031 exchange, which many flippers do not fit in. The key to if you qualify for a 1031 exchange is the reason you purchased your property. For a property to be qualified, it must be purchased and held for trade, investment, or business. This does not include your home, and it prevents properties that were purchased to be sold fast from using a 1031 exchange.

Put simply, a property purchased to be fixed and sold quickly, will fail when it gets investigated by the IRS. However, you are eligible for this tax-deferred strategy in a situation where you purchase a property, hold it for more than a year, and rent it to tenants. But, you will still be eligible if you can purchase a residential property or home, renovate it and hold it for over a year. This way, you will be able to develop your wealth while paying less taxes.

Self-Directed IRA

It may be news to many investors that flipping homes with self-directed IRA funds is possible. Since the individual Retirement Account(IRA) was created, the IRS gave IRA holders the authority to utilize IRA funds in purchasing a home, holding it, or flipping properties.

When you leverage a Self-Directed IRA for the purchase of real estate, you can buy:

- Properties to flip

- Commercial or residential property

- Foreign or domestic real estate

- Undeveloped land

As the owner of a Self-directed IRA, you have complete control and access to your retirement funds. It is known as checkbook control. It gives you the chance to partake in real estate deals without the consent of a custodian. What this implies, is that you can utilize your IRA to purchase a rehab property as simple as writing a check.

A major benefit of checkbook control is; when you are ready to buy a property using your self-directed IRA, you can buy, pay for upgrades and flip the home yourself without the need for an IRA custodian or a financial institution that secures your assets. Similar to the first option above, you can use this to develop your wealth without having to spend too much on taxes.

The strategies above will ensure you can develop your wealth and plan for a comfortable retirement. Regardless of how much you earn, you won't be able to attain financial growth fast if you don't keep a huge part of it, which is what these strategies above can help you do.

Conclusion

Being a home rehabber offers a lot of possibilities. But, you need to note that some risks come with it. Do not go into property rehabbing without proper preparation as it can lead to huge loss of cash.

I have offered you all the data you need in this book. All that is left for you is to go through the information, read, and implement it effectively to ensure the process goes smoothly, and with time, you will be a leader in the business.

So why wait? Take the step now.

Bibliography

Priyanka Prakash, J. (2019). Fix and Flip Loans: How to Get Funding for Flipping Houses. Retrieved from https://www.fundera.com/blog/fix-and-flip-loans

Johnson, D. (2019). 9 Incredibly Important Do's and Don'ts of Flipping Houses. Retrieved from https://www.biggerpockets.com/blog/2013/05/29/important-dos-and-donts-flipping-houses/

Flipping a House? 5 Dos and 5 Don'ts You Need to Know First. (2019). Retrieved from https://www.hgtv.com/shows/flipping-virgins/house-flipping-dos-donts-from-egypt-sherrod

Williams, J. (2019). Flipping Houses 101: The Fundamentals of Flipping Houses. Retrieved from http://houseflippinghq.com/flipping-houses-101-fundamentals/

McWhinney, J. (2019). 5 Mistakes That Can Make House Flipping a Flop. Retrieved from https://www.investopedia.com/articles/mortgages-real-estate/08/house-flip.asp

Bethell, A. (2018). How to Start Your Own House Flipping Business in 6 Steps. Retrieved from https://fitsmallbusiness.com/how-to-start-your-own-house-flipping-business/

Levin, H. (2019). Flipping Houses for Profit - Tips for How to Flip a House. Retrieved from https://www.moneycrashers.com/five-tips-for-effectively-flipping-a-house/

R, R., & Kraynak, J. (2019). Flipping Houses For Dummies Cheat Sheet - dummies. Retrieved from https://www.dummies.com/personal-finance/real-estate-investing/flipping-houses/flipping-houses-for-dummies-cheat-sheet/

House Flipping Basics. (2019). Retrieved from https://homeguides.sfgate.com/house-flipping-basics-6574.html

Goldstein, D. (2016). 6 things to know before you flip a house. Retrieved from https://www.marketwatch.com/story/6-things-to-know-before-you-flip-a-house-2016-07-14

·

www.ingramcontent.com/pod-product-compliance
Lightning Source LLC
Chambersburg PA
CBHW060859170526
45158CB00001B/414